Annika S.
8b

Spanish Gold

A Cornish Treasure Hunt

Philip Hewitt

Cornelsen

Cornelsen English Library

Verlagsredaktion
Dr. Blanca-Maria Rudhart

Umschlaggestaltung
Heike Börner, dia

Titelbilder
Hemera Technologies/Alamy
Corel Library

Illustration
Michael Fleischmann

Typografie
Anna Bakalović und Annika Preyhs, Berlin

Technische Umsetzung
Ingo Ostermaier

www.cornelsen.de

1. Auflage, 1. Druck 2007

Alle Drucke dieser Auflage sind inhaltlich unverändert und können im Unterricht nebeneinander verwendet werden.

Druck: CS-Druck CornelsenStürtz, Berlin

ISBN 978-3-464-31013-7

Inhalt gedruckt auf säurefreiem Papier aus nachhaltiger Forstwirtschaft.

Contents

Chapter 1 Grandad's story

"A big black wooden box full of gold coins," said old Mr Martinez to his surprised grandchildren Andrew and Liz as they sat in front of the warm fire on a cold October evening. "Spanish gold! Thousands of gold Spanish doubloons. The family treasure!"

"How long ago was this?" asked Liz.

"Over four hundred years ago. When the Spanish Armada came across to conquer England."

"That was in 1588," said Andrew, who was good at history at school.

"What happened, Grandad?" asked Liz, who was more interested in the story than in history.

"Well, the King of Spain was so sure that his great Armada would be too much for the English navy that many Spanish noblemen came over on the ships – most of them as officers. The king had promised them land and big houses in England, so many of them had brought soldiers and money with them. Money to pay the soldiers and to buy the things which they needed."

"And the Armada didn't beat the English navy, did they, Grandad?"

"No, Andrew. Sir Francis Drake chased the Spaniards all the way up the English Channel. There were storms and high winds which drove the ships all the way round England and Scotland, then down past Ireland on their long way back home to Spain. Many of the ships never got back. The storms drove them onto the rocks on the coast. Many Spanish sailors and noblemen never saw their homes or country again. And one of them was Alfonso Martinez."

"But that's our name!" cried Liz.

"Of course it is!" replied her grandfather. "And I'm surprised that your father hasn't told you more about your own family history, young lady! Our ancestors were Spanish grandees from Castile. Alfonso was luckier than most of those Spaniards. His ship came on the rocks right here, in North Cornwall."

Liz's eyes opened wide. "Right here?"

"Yes, right here in Portreath. He and the men from his ship brought what they could from the ship before it sank. Then they made their homes here in Cornwall."

"But wasn't England at war with Spain at that time? Didn't they become prisoners of war or something?" asked Andrew.

His grandfather laughed. "Cornwall was not England in those days," he said, "and there were no passports. To a Cornishman four hundred years ago, a Spaniard was not much stranger than an Englishman. Most people in Cornwall still spoke the old language in those days."

"Which old language was that?" asked Andrew.

"Cornish – Kernewek: it was a Celtic language, very similar to Welsh. They called it 'the old language' because it was older than English. But very few people speak Cornish today. In the 16th century, English and Spanish were both foreign languages to most Cornish people. No – if you had money in those days, you were welcome anywhere. Alfonso had brought plenty of money with him – that box full of gold that I was telling you about – so he bought some land and built a big house on the top of the cliffs. He called it Cliff House. The Spanish sailors were good workers. They worked on farms and married local girls. Three or four generations later, their grandchildren and great-grandchildren were as Cornish as the rest of the people. Some of them even changed their names – or never had sons, so the Spanish names were lost. Only old Martinez and his sons kept the old Castilian tradition alive."

"What tradition was that, Grandad?" asked Andrew.

"The house and the land always went to the eldest son."

"Wasn't that very unfair?" asked his granddaughter. "What about the daughters?"

"Well, things were very different four hundred years ago. Women were not emancipated in those days. Boys and girls had different roles."

"But what about the other sons?" asked Andrew. "Surely it was unfair to them, too?"

"Yes," said Mr Martinez. "And that was how the trouble started. For over two hundred years the Martinez family had no trouble with the old tradition. Generation followed generation. When times became difficult for Catholics in England in the 17th century, the family became Protestants and gave their children good Protestant names like Grace, Felicity, Constance for the girls, and Jacob, Jonathan, Reuben for the boys. The oldest son worked on the farm and took it over when his father died. The younger sons became soldiers or sailors or went out to the colonies to make their fortunes. And when they had to leave home, the daughters and the other sons all took their share of the family fortune with them. There was always plenty of gold – Spanish or English – in the big black box which Alfonso had brought from Spain with him."

"Tell us more about the Spanish gold, Grandad!" said Liz.

"Old Alfonso had used much of the money to buy land and build his big house, of course. He was a nobleman, don't forget! But he and his Spanish friends worked hard on the land.

People say that the Martinez family were famous smugglers, too! So there was always plenty of money. Then one day nearly two hundred years ago, the box disappeared."

"Disappeared?"

"Yes – and not only the box. Old Reuben Martinez's eldest son Jonathan disappeared, too. The two eldest Martinez boys were twins, you see. That was really how the trouble started. They were born in 1818, and Jonathan was only twenty minutes older than his brother Aaron. Those twenty minutes made all the difference. The elder twin would get the house and the land, and his twin brother would have to leave home and make his own fortune. As the boys grew up, Aaron began to realize how unfair this was. Although they were brothers – and twin brothers are often very close – they often argued about their situation. Once, when they were still quite young, Aaron nearly killed Jonathan in a fight! So when Aaron was 16, his father sent him away to relatives who had a farm in another part of England, because Aaron had always wanted to become a farmer. Jonathan stayed at home to help his father on the family farm. Reuben Martinez was a good father who loved both his sons, and he was always thinking about a fair way to solve the problem of the twins. At last he found a solution.

"When the twins were 21 years old, their father gave a big party at the old house for his two eldest sons. That was in 1839. After the party, he told Aaron that he had bought some land in America for him. Enough land to start a large farm. This was the best he could do for the younger of the two twins.

"Aaron seemed happy enough, and a few weeks later he left Portreath to start up a farm in Virginia. Then, a few days later, both Jonathan and the box of gold disappeared.

"At the time, everybody thought that Jonathan had stolen the money and left home to start a new life. Reuben tried to find his son, but there was no sign of him anywhere. No news, no letters, nothing.

"Old Reuben lived to a great age, and when he died, in 1862, everybody expected Jonathan to come back to Portreath to claim his inheritance. Notices appeared in all the English newspapers, but nobody answered them. They contacted Aaron, who had a big tobacco plantation in one of the southern states of America and was well known there, but he had no news of his brother, either."

"Did Aaron come home to claim the inheritance?" asked Andrew.

"Of course," his grandfather went on. "He left Charleston by ship and arrived at Plymouth a month later. He wrote to the family lawyer in Redruth that he would be coming in a day or two to claim his inheritance. He took the train from Plymouth to Redruth and went to the lawyer's office the same afternoon. Then, in the early evening, he set off to walk the three miles to Portreath. He could have taken a horse or a carriage, but he decided to walk. He told the lawyer that he would have many things to think about and he wanted to be alone..."

"Go on, Grandad! What happened then?" asked Liz, who loved mystery stories like this.

"He never arrived."

"Never arrived?"

"He disappeared – just like his twin brother all those years before. Nobody in Cornwall ever saw Aaron Martinez alive again."

Chapter 2 Dad's story

Liz and Andrew lived in London. They had been on a visit to their grandfather with their parents over the half-term holiday. When Liz told their father about their grandfather's story, he smiled.

"The old black box full of Spanish gold! That's one of your grandfather's favourite stories. You mustn't believe everything he tells you, Liz."

"Why not? Isn't the story true, Daddy?"

"Well, it's the true story of the Martinez family of Portreath up to 1862. But is this our family?"

"Isn't it?" asked Andrew.

"Your grandad went to live in Portreath when he was quite young," said Mr Martinez. "As far as I know, our family had always lived in the Coventry area. And as far as I know, our family has no connection with the Martinez family in Cornwall except the name. But my father – your grandfather – always believed that there was a connection. He read about Reuben Martinez and his twin sons in a book about Cornwall. Didn't he show you the book?"

"No, he only told us the story," said Liz sadly. "But it was a wonderful story. He made it sound so true!"

"Well, I've got the book. You can both read the story for yourselves. But don't take it too seriously. Your grandfather thinks that Jonathan – the first twin who disappeared – took the money and went to live in Coventry. He didn't want to stay in Cornwall as a farmer. He started his own company. They built bicycles at first, then cars. Your grandfather's great-grandfather was certainly called John, but nobody knows where this John Martinez came from. Perhaps he came from Spain or one of the Spanish colonies and changed his name from Juan to John when he came to live in England. I don't think that there is any connection between the two families. Your grandfather is a dreamer! When Reuben Martinez died, John – if he was the real Jonathan – would have gone down to Cornwall to claim his inheritance."

"But if you lived in Portreath when you were a boy," asked Andrew, "surely you looked for the lost treasure? What happened to Cliff House and the farm anyway?"

"They went to Reuben's eldest daughter Julia. She was married and lived in Bristol. She sold the house and the land. And that was the end of the Martinez's of Portreath!"

"Until Grandad moved back," said Liz slowly.

"That was in the 1950s," their father went on. "By that time Cliff House was a ruin. People said that it was an unlucky house. There were stories of ghosts, and one night about a hundred years ago there was a fire there and the old house burned down. That was the end of Cliff House. Your grandad tried to buy the ruin and some of the land around it from the local farmer, but he wouldn't sell. He said the money would only bring him bad luck."

"Perhaps the farmer thought that the Spanish gold was still in the house somewhere and that he would find it some day," said Andrew, still fascinated by the story.

"Well," their father went on, "one day in the 1970s your granddad bought a metal detector and asked the farmer for permission to look for treasure on his land. We paid the farmer some money and got his permission, and I helped my father look for the missing treasure."

"Did you find anything?" asked Liz with wide eyes.

"We did. Would you like to see what we found?"

"What a question, Dad!"

Mr Martinez went upstairs and came down after a minute or two with a small black box. He put it down on the table.

"Go on, Liz! Open it!" he said with a smile.

Liz opened the box. She took out four small round pieces of metal and three old coins.

"What are these, Dad?"

"The round things are musket balls – bullets from old hunting guns. They're about two hundred years old."

"And the coins?"

"The big one is a Queen Victoria penny. Well over a hundred years old now. But when I was a boy you could still find them in your change if you were lucky. The smaller coin is a King George VI halfpenny from 1939. That could have dropped out of any girl's or boy's trouser pocket in the 1960s. It's not very valuable."

"And the third coin – the very small one?" asked Andrew with interest.

"That," said their father, "is the most valuable coin of all. It's a silver Spanish escudo. Very old and worn. You can't read the date, but it's sixteenth or seventeenth century. That's all that we found."

"No gold? No doubloons?"

"No. No Spanish gold. Only this. Are you disappointed?"

"Not really," said Liz. "But I expect your father was, Dad!"

"Yes. He stopped looking for the treasure after we had found these things. There was nothing else to find, he said. He gave me everything we found and never talked to me about the treasure again."

"But he told us about it!" said Andrew.

His father put his hand on his son's shoulder and smiled. "He told you two a story which he wanted to believe, Andrew. You and Liz are the next generation of Martinez's. He probably told you the story because he thought I wouldn't. And he was right. We're living in the 21st century and should forget about the past. And gold can be a terrible thing," Mr Martinez put his other arm around his daughter's shoulders. "Men will kill for gold. Gold makes people do terrible things sometimes. Never forget that. Gold can drive men mad."

Chapter 3 Easter at Portreath

School started again at the end of October, and Liz and Andrew were too busy to think about their grandfather's story of Spanish gold.

Christmas came and went. Then school again, but a week before the Easter school holidays, their mother got a letter from Cornwall.

"How nice of your grandfather!" she cried. "He's invited you down to Portreath for the Easter holidays on your own! Would you like to go? I think you're both old enough to look after yourselves."

"Can't you and Dad come with us?" asked Liz.

"Well, we can drive you down and stay for a weekend. And we can do the same when we come to fetch you. But I don't think your dad and I can take time off work."

So that is what they did.

*

Old Mr Martinez had a big house in Portreath village near the sea.

"Too big for just me!" he told Liz and Andrew when they arrived there with their parents the weekend before Easter. "I'm always happier when I have visitors. I'm glad that you could all come."

"The weather is fine, too," said their mum. "We aren't always so lucky."

"Tell us the story about the Spanish gold again!" begged Liz.

"Not now, my dear," said old Mr Martinez, looking quickly at his son. "Later, perhaps. Now it's time for tea."

The family had a wonderful weekend together. The weather was warm and they spent a lot of time on the beach. On Sunday afternoon Mr and Mrs Martinez had to drive back to London. Back to work on Monday! Before they left, Mr Martinez had a word with Andrew.

"Enjoy yourselves – but don't ask your grandad to tell you too many stories about the old days. It sometimes upsets him. You're nearly thirteen now, and Liz is fourteen. Have a good time, but don't do anything silly."

"We won't, Dad," said Andrew, wondering what his father meant. "You can trust us."

"I know I can," said his dad. "But enjoy yourselves anyway!"

*

"What shall we do this morning?" asked Liz on the first day of their holiday.

"It's a nice day," said Andrew. "Let's just go for a walk around the village."

They walked down to the beach and along the pier. From the end of the pier they had a fine view of the rocks which the Spanish ship had hit all those years ago. Even on this warm spring morning the Atlantic waves were crashing heavily on the rocks.

"Let's walk to the top of the cliffs," suggested Liz. "Perhaps we can find Cliff House, the old home of the Martinez family."

"Good idea. But we don't know where it is, do we?"

"Shall we ask Grandad?"

"No. Remember what Dad said. It might upset him. We shouldn't talk too much about family history. The big cliff is over there on the other side of the river. Let's walk to the top and see if we can see the ruins of an old house."

It was a long walk, and they were quite tired when they reached the top of the cliff. The view was wonderful, but there was no sign of a house or even the ruin of a house. What they found was a small airfield with a high fence around it.

Liz looked at Andrew. "What now?"

"Perhaps the house was on the cliff on the other side of the beach."

"We could ask somebody."

"But there's nobody here," said Andrew. "Let's go down and ask in the village. Maybe somebody there will know. We can ask the man in the Post Office. I expect he knows everything about everybody!"

"Good idea."

Just as they were walking back to the village, they saw a small plane flying towards them. It flew low over their heads and landed at the airfield.

"That looks like fun!" said Andrew.

"I wonder who uses this airfield," said Liz.

"Maybe the postmaster knows that, too. Let's ask him."

They walked back down the hill to the village.

Luckily there was nobody in the Post Office when they arrived, so the friendly old postmaster had time to answer their questions.

"Cliff House was up on the cliff where the airfield is now, but they pulled the house down nearly thirty years ago and used the stones to build the new buildings on the airfield when it was an RAF station. It was good stone, you see. Too good to waste. When I was a boy – that's over fifty years ago – we used to play in the ruins of Cliff House. It was a strange place, and we only played there in the sunshine. We never went near the place at night or when there was mist or fog."

"Why not?" asked Liz.

He did not answer at once because a woman had come into the Post Office for some stamps. When the customer had gone, the old postmaster smiled and said: "Because of the ghosts, young lady!"

"Ghosts?"

"The old people said that there were ghosts in the old house. Nobody had lived there for over a hundred years. Something terrible happened there. I don't remember what it was."

"The Martinez twins," said Andrew simply. "They both disappeared."

The old postmaster stopped smiling and looked sharply at Andrew.

"What do you know about that, young man?"

"Our name is Martinez, too," said Liz. "Our family comes from Coventry and we live in London now, but our grandfather thinks that we have some connection to the Martinez family that lived here a long time ago."

"Ah!" said the postmaster. "You must be Jon Martinez's grandchildren!"

"That's right. We're spending our Easter holidays with him," said Liz. "Do you know him?"

"Everybody in the village knows Jon Martinez," said the postmaster with a smile. "My children went to school with your father! I remember your dad very well. He was a friend of my son's. A fine, hard-working boy at school. But don't believe everything your grandfather tells you about his 'family'! Jon Martinez is just a dreamer!"

They bought some stamps and a couple of picture postcards of the village, then went outside to write them.

"He called grandad a dreamer," said Liz slowly. "That's what Daddy called him. I wonder why?"

"Perhaps because he wants something that he can't get. That's what people usually mean when they call other people dreamers. He's dreaming about some connection between the old Martinez family and our family."

"Perhaps he's still dreaming about finding the Spanish gold!" suggested Liz.

"I wish you'd stop talking about that," said Andrew almost angrily. "Remember what Dad said about gold. It drives people mad."

"But just imagine!" his sister went on. "Just imagine finding it!"

Chapter 4 Seek and you shall find

"I've got a surprise for you today," said Mr Martinez at breakfast the following morning.

"What is it, Grandad?" asked Liz.

"If I tell you what it is, young lady, it won't be a surprise! But you will need warm pullovers and don't forget to bring your cameras!"

They got into their grandad's car and drove off through the village and up Lighthouse Hill towards the airfield which the children had seen the day before.

At the top of the hill they turned right along the high fence and then left through an open gate and past a big notice with the words WEDDELL AIR SERVICES.

They stopped outside a large stone building near the edge of the cliffs.

"This is where Cliff House stood," said their grandfather. "They used the stones from the old ruin for this building. This is all that's left of the old house."

There was a sign with the word OFFICE above the door. They got out of the car and a young man of about thirty came out of the office to meet them.

"This is my friend Johnny Weddell," said Mr Martinez, turning to him, "and these are my grandchildren Elizabeth and Andrew."

They shook hands. Liz liked Johnny Weddell. He had short black hair and a friendly smile.

"Are you ready for your flight?" he asked them.

"Flight?" cried Liz in surprise.

"Yes. Your grandfather's booked a flight to Lands End for you today. I'm your pilot. Put your pullovers on now. It's cold up there!"

He locked the door to the office and they walked over to a small four-seater plane which was standing on the runway. Liz was very excited. She was allowed to sit next to the pilot. Andrew and Mr Martinez sat behind them. The plane took off into the wind and five minutes later they were flying back over the airfield and high above Portreath.

They flew south-west over Camborne and Hayle. Just before they reached Penzance, Johnny took the plane quite low over St Michael's Mount so that they could see the castle and church on top of this high rocky island just off the coast.

Then they flew west over the little town of Penzance towards the south-western tip of England: Lands End.

Andrew looked down at the rocky coast where the Atlantic waves were crashing against the cliffs and realized why so many ships of the Spanish Armada had never got back to Spain.

"The weather is good," said the pilot. "Shall we go on to the Scilly Islands?"

"Yes, please, Mr Weddell!" said Liz.

"Call me Johnny," he said. "Everybody does."

Mr Martinez smiled. He was enjoying his flight, too.

"Where are the Islands?" asked Liz. "I can't see them."

"The Scillies? They're about thirty miles away," said Johnny. "You'll be able to see them in a few minutes."

They flew on across the deep greenish blue of the Atlantic and soon they could see a group of islands ahead. Two or three were quite big, the others were small or very small – just rocks in the sea.

"The biggest island is St Mary's," said Johnny. "That's where most people live. We'll fly over the capital, Hugh Town, so you can take a few photos. Then we'll turn back."

Half an hour later they landed back at Portreath airfield. They got out of the plane and thanked Johnny and their grandfather for a wonderful morning.

Johnny Weddell smiled. "My pleasure!"

Andrew was interested in the pilot's work. "Do you just take tourists for flights to Lands End?"

"No. I couldn't live from tourism, Andrew. I do a lot of work for farmers: crop-spraying and things like that. There are one or two local businessmen who want to go somewhere in a hurry. If you're interested in planes or flying, you can come up and have a look around any time."

"Do you fly at night, too?"

"No. The airfield hasn't got the equipment for night flights. No runway lights. And we're too close to the cliffs. It would be too dangerous to take off or land at night."

They said goodbye to the friendly pilot and drove back to the village.

In the afternoon, Mr Martinez took the children to St Mary's Church in Portreath to see the 'family graves' as he called them.

"Most of the old Martinez family are buried here," he told them as they walked from grave to grave, looking at the names and dates on them. "I know that your father thinks that we have no connection with this Martinez family, but I like to think that we do."

"Some of them died very young," said Liz. "This little girl was only eight years old! That's six years younger than me!"

"Many children died young in the old days," said her grandfather, "but old Reuben lived to a great age. That's his grave over there."

They walked over to what looked like a big stone box almost a metre high. They read the words on the lid:

> In loving memory of
>
> **Reuben James Martinez**
>
> Cliff House, Portreath.
> Born there on 26th February 1775.
> Died there on 10th April 1862.
>
> *
>
> "Seek not my gold below this stone!
> No treasure could I take with me.
> Here lie my fleshless bones alone,
> and my lost son beyond the sea!
> Nothing have I left behind.
> Only seek and you shall find."

"What strange things to put on a grave!" said Liz. "What does it all mean, Grandad?"

"I wish I knew what it means!" said Mr Martinez. "I've been thinking about the meaning of those words for over thirty years. The first line is a warning not to open the grave. That's clear enough."

"But it seems to say that there is still some gold, but that it is somewhere else – not here," said Andrew quietly.

"If there really is any gold. Perhaps the word 'gold' just means 'money'. And the second line is clear enough: when you die, you can't take anything with you."

"And the third and fourth lines sound as if he was expecting his son in America to come back and look for some sort of treasure!" Liz went on.

"But surely Jonathan had already stolen the treasure and disappeared. He had probably even left England – so maybe he is the 'lost son beyond the sea'. Aaron was farming in America. He wasn't lost! Perhaps Reuben even knew where Jonathan was. It looks as if he were asking him to come back and look for something else, not just the family treasure."

"But only Aaron came back," said Liz. "And he only got as far as Redruth, didn't he? Then he disappeared. How strange!"

She sat down on the grave and began to think.

"The fifth line makes no sense, does it, Grandad?" said Andrew. "He left everything behind! He couldn't take anything with him. He says so in the second line, doesn't he?"

"Yes, that's the big mystery. If he left nothing behind, why should somebody seek something that isn't there?"

There was silence for a minute before Mr Martinez spoke. "I think Reuben left this message for his sons – or for one of them. He wanted them to look for something that was not part of their inheritance when they came back to Cliff House."

"The Spanish gold," said Liz suddenly. "That must be it! It didn't disappear when Jonathan disappeared. Aaron came back to Cliff House before he went to America and killed his twin brother. They had a fight about the family treasure and Aaron killed Jonathan. How terrible! Reuben found out what had happened. He kept the gold but had to send Aaron away again – because if the police had caught him, they would have hanged him. And both Reuben's sons would have been dead long before he died. He didn't want Aaron to have the gold. The gold had belonged to Jonathan and now Jonathan was dead. Aaron would have to look for it after Reuben's death – and perhaps he would never find it. Because it might be in a place where he would never think of looking – or never dare to look! Perhaps Reuben buried it near Jonathan's body. After all, the gold would have been Jonathan's. It belonged with him if not to him!"

She stopped and looked up at her brother and grandfather, who were both staring at her in astonishment.

"What's the matter?" she asked in surprise.

"What on earth are you saying, child?" asked Mr Martinez, shocked. "What gave you those ideas?"

"Which ideas?"

"What you were just saying: about Aaron killing Jonathan, and Reuben burying the treasure beside his son's body before he died and making Aaron look for it everywhere except where it was really buried..."

It was Liz's turn to look astonished now. She jumped off the lid of Reuben's grave as if the stone had burned her.

"I don't remember saying that!" she cried, staring first at her grandfather, then at her brother. "I don't remember saying anything! I was thinking – but not about that! I never said anything like that!"

She sat slowly back down on the lid of old Reuben's grave and began to cry.

Chapter 5 The missing tower

"It was the voice of old Reuben Martinez speaking through young Elizabeth," said Mr Martinez to Andrew later that evening. They had put Liz to bed early with a cup of hot milk and an aspirin. The poor girl was still very upset.

"Surely you don't believe that, Grandad!" said Andrew.

"She was sitting on Reuben's grave when she spoke. And she couldn't remember saying anything. It's all very strange. I think your sister has at last discovered what really happened all those years ago."

Andrew looked closely at his grandfather. The old man was looking down at the table. What was he thinking about? Did he really think that Reuben had spoken through Liz? That was a crazy idea – a mad idea.

"What I don't understand," said Andrew, "is why Aaron never came back to Cliff House. Why he disappeared."

"Perhaps he went to see his father's grave before going up to the house," said Mr Martinez slowly. "Perhaps he read the message on the grave, understood it, and then went straight to the place where he had left Jonathan's body. If he found the gold, he would have to tell people where he had found it. Then they would find Jonathan's body and know what must have happened. Perhaps he thought it would be better to take the treasure and go straight back to America. Perhaps that's why he never went to the house – because Jonathan's body was somewhere else!"

"It's too fantastic, Grandad," said Andrew. "I don't believe that's what happened at all."

"Just one thing, Andrew. Please don't tell your parents about what happened today. They might be upset. They might even want you both to go back home, and that would spoil your Easter holiday, wouldn't it?"

"OK, Grandad," said Andrew. Later he wished he had not given his promise. Because he had never seen his grandfather's eyes shining in that way before.

He remembered what his father had told him about gold driving people mad.

*

The next morning Liz seemed quite happy and normal. They had breakfast, and Mr Martinez suggested a trip to Truro, the old capital of Cornwall. He talked to the children a lot on the way there, pointing to interesting places which they passed and telling them about spring in the countryside. Andrew and Liz lived in a big city, of course, so they were very interested.

They walked around the centre of town looking at the shops and other interesting buildings. After lunch, Mr Martinez took them to the museum. Liz and Andrew didn't really like museums much, but Truro Museum had a special section for children with a lot of interesting photos of Cornwall. There was a big glass case full of old coins.

"Those are gold Spanish doubloons from one of the Armada ships," Mr Martinez showed them. "Aren't they beautiful?"

They certainly were beautiful: over four hundred years old and still a bright orange-yellow colour. But to Andrew they looked strange, almost alien, beside the simple silver coins of his own country. The idea of the Spanish Armada, the strangers who had wanted to conquer his country so long ago, with their strange language, customs and bright coins made of gold stolen from the Indians of their South American colonies was something which somehow worried Andrew. Something seemed to be worrying Liz, too. She was standing in front of some photos of towns and villages in the area.

"Grandad!" she called over to them. "Isn't this Cliff House?"

Mr Martinez walked over to the wall and put his arm around Liz's shoulders. "It is, my dear," he said, after looking at the photo for some seconds. "But how did you know?"

"Oh! Daddy must have shown me a photo of it in the old days, before it burned down."

"Ah, yes. I see," said her grandfather quietly.

But Andrew did not 'see' at all. He had certainly never seen a photo of Cliff House except as a ruin. At least his father had never shown him any. Why should his sister know more about the old family home than he did? But of course it was not the old family home. The Martinez family had come from Coventry. The only connection was the name.

But the more time Andrew spent with his grandfather in Portreath, the more often he had to tell himself that there was no connection – there was no connection at all… only the name… Martinez.

"What a big house it was," Liz went on, still looking at the photo. Andrew looked at it more closely now, and read what was written under the picture: '1880 – Many rich Cornish families lived in big houses like this one'. It did not say: 'This is Cliff House, Portreath, home of the Martinez family'. How did Liz know? He listened, fascinated, as she talked about the old house as if she had once lived there! "You can't see the farm buildings because they're at the back of the house. But here's the summerhouse and the coach house, and here's…"

She stopped. She was pointing at a part of the photo where there was nothing to see – just grass at the top of the cliff behind the house. She turned round to her grandfather, staring with wide eyes.

"It's not there, Grandad!"

"What's not there, Elizabeth?"

She looked back at the photo and thought for a moment. "I don't know," she said at last. "I just had a sudden feeling that there should be another building here, but there isn't."

Mr Martinez said nothing. They walked around the rest of the museum, but somehow Andrew was glad when they were outside in the warm spring sunshine again.

On the way back to Portreath, Mr Martinez hardly spoke at all. When Andrew asked him about the places they were driving past, he sometimes had to ask the same question twice. His grandfather was thinking about something else all the time.

After tea, Liz and Andrew walked down to the beach. Liz was very quiet.

"What's wrong, Liz?" her brother asked.

"Wrong? Nothing's wrong. Why?"

"You're very quiet today. I was wondering if you were worried about something, that's all."

"No."

They walked on for a while in silence before Liz spoke again.

"Well, there is something that's worrying me. I had a strange dream last night. I was walking up Lighthouse Hill towards Cliff House. It was night. The house looked just like the one on the photo in the museum, but on the cliff behind the house was a high tower. The house was dark but there was a light at the top of the tower. I didn't go towards the house.

I walked straight up to the tower. The door at the bottom was open. I went in. Then I started to walk up the stone stairs towards the room at the top of the tower… Oh, Andrew! I knew that there was something terrible in that room, but I couldn't stop myself from walking up the stairs. There was light coming from under the door at the top of the stairs. I walked up to the door and put my hand on it. I couldn't stop myself, Andrew, even though I was so frightened and I thought that if I opened that door, I would surely die…"

"And? What was behind the door? What was in the room, Liz?"

"Nothing."

"Nothing?"

"There was no room behind the door, Andrew! Just the wild sea! The light I had seen was daylight. And suddenly there was no tower, either. I felt myself falling. Then I woke up."

"Why didn't you tell us about your dream at breakfast? I'm sure that Grandad…"

"That's just it, Andrew. You must promise me not to tell Grandad about my dream. I don't want him to know anything about it. He's our grandfather and I love him, but yesterday and today he has looked at me in a strange way that frightens me, Andrew! It's the family treasure, the Spanish gold – he wants the gold so badly, and he thinks I know where it is… or how to find it. He frightens me! Don't tell him about my dream or about the tower!"

"But there is no tower, Liz. You saw the photo in the museum."

"There was a tower in my dream. And maybe there was a tower there years before that photo. We must find out if there was. Who would know – apart from Grandad, of course?"

"Perhaps we could ask the postmaster again," said Andrew. "Let's walk back to the Post Office. It should still be open."

It was, and the postmaster was very helpful. He had a book about the history of the area with lots of photos. He told Liz and Andrew about the tower.

"The tower was as old as the house. Four hundred years old at least. On dark stormy nights they used it as a lighthouse to warn ships to stay away from the rocks. That was before they built the lighthouse at the top of Lighthouse Hill. But the tower was too close to the edge of the cliff. The sea is always cutting into the cliffs along the coast, and one stormy night, the rocks on which the tower stood fell into the sea, and the tower fell with it. That was in the 1850s, when old Reuben Martinez was still alive. There was a lot of smuggling in Cornwall in the old days, and the Martinez family were famous smugglers! People say that there was a secret tunnel from the tower down to a cave on the beach and another tunnel from the tower to the house itself, so the smugglers could move smuggled goods from the cave to the house without anyone seeing them, but the tunnel to the cave disappeared when the tower fell, of course. It all fell into the cave below!"

"And the tunnel to the house?" asked Liz.

The postmaster turned over a few pages in his book, but there was nothing in the book about secret tunnels.

"I suppose the tunnel – or part of it – must still be there," said the postmaster. "But the house is gone now, so we'll never know, will we?"

They left the Post Office and walked back to the beach. Liz was strangely quiet again.

"What's the matter, Liz?" asked Andrew.

"The new building on the airfield is where Cliff House stood. Perhaps the tunnel is still under it. Maybe we can ask Johnny Weddell about it."

"What's so important about the tunnel?"

"I'm not sure," she said. "But I think I'll know more about the tunnel soon."

Andrew did not ask his sister why. He already knew what to expect. Liz was going to have another of her strange dreams.

Chapter 6 Two strange dreams

Most of us have dreams at some time or another. Sometimes we have nice dreams. Sometimes we have bad dreams.

But Liz sometimes had strange dreams about the future. Dreams which came true. She did not often talk to people about her dreams, but usually she told her brother. Because he sometimes had the same sort of dream.

It was night – Liz hated dreams about night, where everything was dark – and she was walking up a hill. There was nothing at the top of the hill. No buildings, no Cliff House. In front of her was a long straight road. It seemed to go on and on for ever, and it was very wide. She started to walk along it. Far away behind her she suddenly heard a noise. The noise of a car. No, it wasn't a car. It was a small plane. And suddenly she knew where she was. She was walking along the runway of the airfield at Portreath. The plane was coming closer. If she didn't get out of the way, it would hit her! She began to run, but she did not run to the side. Somehow she could not make her legs move to the left or to the right – she went on running straight on, down the runway. And the plane was right behind her now. Any second now it would hit her!

Suddenly she was falling. There was a hole in the runway, and she had fallen into it. The plane flew over the top of her and was gone. The hole above her closed and she was in the dark. She hated the dark. She held out her arms and turned around. There were walls on both sides of her but nothing in front of or behind her. So she must be in a tunnel. She had to find her way out of the tunnel. Which way? Then she saw that there was a light at one end of the tunnel, so she began to walk towards it. She could not walk fast because now she was carrying something very heavy. What was it? As the light from the end of the tunnel got brighter, she could finally see what she was carrying.

It was a heavy black wooden box.

Liz was very frightened now. The light at the end of the tunnel was not daylight or moonlight or electric light. It was a candle standing on a chair in the middle of a room – not a room, she thought. A cellar. There was somebody moving about in the cellar. She could see a shadow on the wall. She stopped and watched. A tall man with a big black beard came up to the opening where the tunnel entered the cellar and put down a large square stone against one of the walls. He disappeared for a few seconds and came back with another big stone. Then another. And a fourth. The four large stones filled the bottom of the opening from wall to wall. What was he doing? He brought four more stones one after another and put them on top of the first four. Suddenly Liz realized what he was doing: he was building a wall.

He went away for more stones. Liz watched, more fascinated than frightened at first. But the wall was quite high now, and she wanted to cry out, to tell him to stop, to ask him to let her out. But no cry came. Only four more big heavy stones. The next four almost filled the opening. She tried to move – to run forward – but she couldn't. She wanted to drop the heavy box, but she couldn't. She tried to cry out again, but she couldn't. Slowly the tall man with the big black beard put the top four stones in the opening and the light from the candle disappeared.

Liz was alone again in the dark.

Buried alive.

*

Andrew had a strange dream that night, too. He was up in a small plane with Johnny Weddell. They were flying up and down the Cornish coast. It was a beautiful day. But where was Liz? They always went everywhere together. Why wasn't she up in the plane with them?

Then he looked down and saw her. She was standing at the top of a pile of rocks high up on the cliff, waving to the plane. He waved back. The heavy Atlantic waves were crashing against the bottom of the cliff. Suddenly the rocks at the bottom of the cliff began to move. The whole side of the cliff began to slide into the sea. Andrew wanted to cry out – to warn Liz, but no cry came. She was still waving to them when the pile of rocks which she was standing on began to slide slowly down into the sea. Liz did not move – she went on waving until...

Andrew woke up with the cry still on his lips.

The terrible picture of the sliding cliff was gone, but he could still hear the plane. Then he realized that it was the sound of a real plane, quite loud and not far away. It was coming in to land.

Strange, he thought. Johnny told us that they don't fly at night. They haven't got the equipment. No runway lights...

The noise of the plane stopped, and Andrew went back to sleep.

Chapter 7 Ghost hunt

The following morning Mr Martinez had to go to Truro. He asked Andrew and Liz if they wanted to come with him, but they said they wanted to stay in Portreath. It was another lovely morning, and they wanted to go down to the beach and watch the fishing boats in the harbour.

"I'll probably be home at lunch-time," said Mr Martinez, "but if I'm not back by two o'clock, you can make yourselves a sandwich or something. There's plenty of food in the fridge. You'll be OK on your own, won't you?"

"Don't worry, Grandad," said Liz with a big smile. "We'll be fine! We're old enough to look after ourselves. Enjoy yourself in Truro!"

When he had driven off in the car, Liz turned to Andrew and asked, almost as if she already knew the answer: "We're not going down to the beach, are we?"

"No," replied her brother. "We're going to the airfield to see if Johnny Weddell needs any help."

"Help?"

"Well, we must have an excuse for visiting him. We can tell him that we're very interested in planes. Maybe we can wash the office windows or something. Anything to give us a chance to have a good look around. Something strange is going on up there, Liz. I heard a plane land there last night. At first I thought that I was dreaming, but the noise woke me up. It was real enough. And it was the middle of the night. He told us that they don't fly at night. And why should they? They can't go crop-spraying in the dark!"

"I don't like it up there at the airfield," Liz began. "I had a strange dream about a plane last night, too."

She told Andrew her dream.

"Well," he said, "that gives us another good reason to find out what's going on up there. He said we could come up and look around the airfield any time, didn't he? Come on, Liz. It'll be fun!"

So they walked up Lighthouse Hill to the airfield.

Johnny Weddell was busy talking to a man who was loading several large brown-paper parcels into his car.

"Hello, you two!" Johnny called out to them. "Just go into the office for a minute while we finish loading up."

"Can we help?" asked Liz.

"Not with this job!" said Johnny with a smile. "I'll be with you in a minute. Help yourselves to a bottle of Coke. There's plenty in the office."

They went inside and found their drinks. Andrew went over to the window and was watching the man loading the van. The man picked up the last parcel and threw it into the back of his car. It slipped off the seat onto the ground and the brown paper tore open.

Several small green packets slipped out of the parcel.

"Be a bit more careful!" cried Johnny to the man, quickly picking the packets up, throwing them into the car and closing the door. "You don't want anyone to see what you've got in there, do you?"

Andrew looked away quickly and moved away from the window before Johnny could see him.

Andrew did not smoke, of course, but he knew what was in the parcels: his father made his own cigarettes with that brand of tobacco. 50 grams cost £12 in British shops or only £5 if you knew someone who 'brought it in' from Belgium or Luxemburg, where it cost about £2.75.

So smuggling in Cornwall was not dead! Andrew wondered if there was a connection between the plane which had landed here in the night and these brown-paper parcels. Probably. He wished he hadn't seen what he had seen and hoped that Johnny had not noticed that he had been watching.

When Johnny Weddell came into the office, he was smiling.

"I expect you want to look around a bit," he said. "I'll show you the planes if you like."

He spent the next hour showing Liz and Andrew around the planes and buildings, telling them all about Weddell Air Services. Andrew found it all very interesting and asked Johnny a lot of questions about his work, but Liz seemed a bit bored – no, not exactly bored, thought Andrew. His sister seemed to be waiting for something more important to happen. While they had been waiting in the office, she had walked around the room as if she were looking for something.

"I think I've shown you everything now," Johnny finally said, as he took them back to the office for another Coke.

It was then that Liz began to show more interest. The first thing she asked about was the toilets.

"The 'Ladies' is down the corridor on the right," said Johnny. "I'm sorry, Liz! I should have asked you if you needed to use the 'rest room' as the Americans call it. I hope it's clean enough! We don't get many lady visitors here!"

Liz was away for almost ten minutes.

"I hope she hasn't lost her way!" laughed Johnny. But Andrew noticed that he kept looking over at the door to the corridor as if he were worried about something else.

When Liz finally came back she took her Coke and sat down. Now it was her turn to ask a few questions.

"You told us that this building is right on top of the old Cliff House. Is that right?"

"Yes. Some of the walls and many of the stones are actually from the old house itself. It's good stone. Too good to waste."

"The floors aren't new, are they?"

"No," said Johnny. "But they were the best part of the old building. The RAF kept the floors and built this building around them. To save money, I suppose."

"So the cellars of the old house are still there?"

Weddell looked at Liz strangely for a few seconds before replying.

"The cellars? Yes, they're still there. But we don't use them – we don't need them, Liz. Weddell Air Services is only interested in things that are up in the air, not down underground. Why do you ask?"

"I thought that you might have filled the cellars in when you bought the place from the RAF."

"Why would we do that?" asked Johnny in surprise.

"Because of the ghosts, of course!"

"Ghosts?" said Weddell – quite sharply, Andrew thought. "There are no ghosts here, young lady!"

"Oh yes there are," said Liz quite seriously. "I know that there are. I can feel things like that! There's at least one ghost downstairs in your cellars." Then, in her sweetest voice, she asked her big question: "Will you show us the cellars, please, Johnny? I'd love to go down there! I want to see if I'm right about the ghost!"

Johnny Weddell was so surprised that he did not know what to say.

So Liz went on: "You aren't afraid of ghosts, are you, Johnny?"

Her voice was still sweet, but her eyes were watching him sharply.

For a few moments, Andrew really thought that Johnny Weddell was going to throw them out, but the young man seemed to suddenly change his mind. He turned to his desk and picked up his keys.

"Come on, then," he said. "Follow me!"

They walked out of the office and down a corridor with doors on both sides. At the end of the corridor was a stone wall with a large door in it. Johnny finally found the right key, turned it and pulled the heavy old door slowly open. Andrew and Liz could see that nobody had opened the door for a long time.

Cold air came up to meet them. Liz shivered a little.

"Are you sure you still want to see the cellars?" Johnny asked with a smile as he switched on the lights. "It's not very warm down there. As I told you, we don't use the cellars. Be careful! The stairs are a bit wet!"

He went down the stairs first. The two young people followed.

"Well," said Andrew as they reached the bottom of the stairs, "if there isn't a ghost in here, there certainly should be. It's an ideal place for ghosts."

He was right. The cellars were high, with round ceilings. There were several rooms, and they were all empty. Johnny had been telling the truth after all. They walked from room to room. There's nothing to see down here, thought Andrew. No piles of smuggled goods. Why on earth had Liz wanted to come down to the cellars? He turned around to ask her, but she was not there.

"Liz? Liz! Where are you?"

She had not followed them into the last room. Where on earth was the girl?

"What's the matter?" asked Johnny.

"Liz must have gone back to one of the other rooms," said Andrew. "She was behind me just now. Liz!"

They found her in the first room. She was standing quite still in the doorway with her back to them, staring at something on the opposite wall. When she heard them coming, she didn't turn round. She just stood there, staring.

"It's there, Andrew! Can you see it!"

"What can you see, Liz?" asked Johnny. "A ghost?"

Andrew looked at the wall. Then he, too, saw it. Not a ghost but a low doorway. A doorway without a door. A doorway blocked with large square stones.

The other side of the doorway in Liz's dream!

Liz turned round to them at last. Her face was quite white.

"Thank you, Johnny," she said. "I've seen all I wanted to see."

And without another word she walked out of the room, up the stairs, along the corridor and out into the bright spring sunshine.

Horrible, she thought. Terrible! But perhaps it's true after all. It was not just a dream.

Chapter 8 On the cliffs

Andrew thanked Johnny Weddell for being so kind to them and apologized for his sister's strange behaviour. Then he ran after her. She was almost at the airfield gate before he caught her up.

"What was all that about?" he asked angrily. "Why did you run off like that? What's the matter with you, Liz!"

"I'm sorry, Andrew. I couldn't stay down there a second longer. You know I don't like dark places."

"But it wasn't dark, Liz. There were bright lights in every room!"

"All I could see was two candles in a dark room and a big man with a long black beard. He was blocking the doorway with big stones. Just like in my dream."

Was his sister going mad? What on earth was she talking about?

"Stop it, Liz! You must stop thinking about that terrible dream of yours!"

"I can't!" she cried, staring at her brother with wide, frightened eyes. "It was so real! I've got to find out the truth! That doorway was the entrance to the old tunnel that led to the tower. Reuben must have blocked it up when the tower fell into the sea. But the tunnel is still there. And there's something in it, Andrew! The terrible secret of the old Martinez family!"

"What terrible secret? What secret, Liz? Speak to me! Tell me!!"

Andrew suddenly realized that he was holding Liz by the shoulders and shaking her. Was he going mad, too? He quickly let go of his sister and waited for her to say something.

"I can't! It's too horrible, Andrew! And I may be wrong – I hope I am. But I don't think so. The only thing that I know is that we have to find out what's behind that wall."

"And how on earth are we going to do that?"

"We'll just have to find the other end of the tunnel, stupid! Come on!"

"Where are we going?"

"To look around the top of the cliffs for the other entrance, of course."

"But it's long past lunch-time, Liz. Grandad will be waiting for us. He'll be worried if we aren't home when he comes back from Truro."

But Liz wasn't listening. She was already marching down the narrow path which led to the cliffs. Andrew followed her.

There was a fence and a big notice at the top of the cliffs: DANGER: LOOSE ROCKS. KEEP OFF! Liz climbed over the fence and began walking towards a big pile of loose rocks. Andrew stopped at the fence and watched her.

"Are you crazy, Liz!" he shouted. "Come back!"

But Liz didn't come back. She went on walking. Climbing up the loose rocks near the top of the cliff until, with a sudden cry, she disappeared.

*

"Liz! Andrew! Are you there?" called Mr Martinez as he walked into the hall of his house. "Have you had lunch yet? I've brought you some fish and chips!"

But there was no answer. He looked at the clock in the hall. It was nearly two o'clock. Where could they be? He had told them he would be back at lunch-time. Perhaps they were still down on the beach. He would just walk down to the beach with their fish and chips and surprise them!

Liz and Andrew were not on the beach. Nor in any of the shops in the village street. Mr Martinez walked back to his house. He was a bit worried now. He put down the fish and chips and picked up the telephone. First he phoned the Post Office. Perhaps his friend Fred, the postmaster, had seen them. Fred sat in his window all day and saw everybody who walked up and down the street.

But the postmaster had not seen his grandchildren.

"They were here yesterday, though," he said. "They seemed very interested in Cliff House. I showed them some photos in my book. They were especially interested in the old tower and the tunnels. Why? Is anything wrong?"

"No," said Mr Martinez, although he thought there was. "What did you tell them about the tower – and the tunnels?"

"I told them what everybody knows. The tunnel to the cave is gone. It went when the tower fell."

"And the other tunnel? The tunnel from the tower to the house?"

"There's nothing about the other tunnel in my book. I suppose it's still there. Johnny Weddell should know. He lives on top of the cliffs where Cliff House used to be. Are you sure that everything's OK?"

"Everything's fine, Fred," said Mr Martinez, although he now knew that it wasn't. "But if you see them walking around the village, tell them I'm home and a bit worried about them."

"I'll certainly do that, Jonathan. 'Bye."

Mr Martinez picked up his briefcase and opened it. He took out the papers that he had brought back from the Public Records Office in Truro. They were drawings – plans of a house and the land around it. Old plans. Plans that he had never seen before. Plans that had taken him thirty years to find. Now at last he had them. They were the plans of Cliff House in the 1850s.

He had wanted to show them to his grandchildren first, but now he could not wait. He had to look at them now. Yes – there was the house and the gardens – and the tower. So the tunnel must be...

The telephone rang. It was Johnny Weddell.

"I just thought I'd tell Liz that she's left her jacket here in my office," he said.

"In your office? You mean Liz and Andrew were up at the airfield this morning?"

"Yes. What's wrong with that? They're very welcome."

"They said they were going down to the beach. When did they leave?"

"About an hour ago. Aren't they home yet?"

"No. Did they tell you where they were going?"

"No, but Liz left in a hurry. I think she was glad to get outside into the fresh air. She wanted to see the cellars, said she was looking for a ghost! I think she was a bit frightened."

"She wanted to see the cellars? She was looking for a ghost?"

"That's right. That's what she said. Is anything wrong?"

"I hope not! Look, I'm coming up right now, Johnny. I've no idea where the children are, and I'm getting a bit worried."

"OK. Come right up. I'll see if they're wandering around on the cliffs outside."

Please God – No! thought Mr Martinez as he took a quick look at the old plans, picked up his car keys and ran out of the house. Just as he was getting into the car, an ambulance drove quickly past, its siren blaring and its blue lights flashing.

Mr Martinez watched it turn left at the end of the road and up Lighthouse Hill towards the airfield. He hid his face in his hands. Suddenly he felt very old and very tired. Driving slowly and carefully, he followed the ambulance up the hill.

*

The paramedics were carrying Andrew to the ambulance when Mr Martinez arrived at the top of the cliffs. The police were there, too. Johnny Weddell was talking to a policewoman who was writing something down in her notebook. Other people were already walking or driving up the hill from the village to see what was happening.

"Andrew!" cried Mr Martinez, running up to the ambulance. But Andrew could not hear him. He was unconscious. The paramedics put Andrew into the ambulance. "What happened? Will he be all right?"

"It's too early to say," said one of the men. "There's been another big rock fall. One of the rocks must have hit him on the head."

"I'm his grandfather. Where are you taking him?"

"Truro General Hospital. Do you want to come with us?"

Mr Martinez looked round quickly. "Where's Elizabeth?"

"Elizabeth?"

"His sister! He was here with his sister! They were always together. Elizabeth!" he called, but there was no reply. He looked at the new pile of stones and rocks in front of him. "Oh, God!" he cried. "Surely not under that?"

*

Even much later, Liz was not sure what really happened. One moment she had been standing on the rocks beside the wall of the cliff, the next moment the pile of rocks had begun to slide and a hole had opened up in the cliff just under her feet. She must have fallen into the hole because the next thing she knew was that she was lying on the hard floor of a dark tunnel. Small stones were still falling around her, and a large rock or something had fallen across the hole and blocked it.

Just like in her dream.

She was alone in the dark tunnel and felt very frightened. She could see nothing.

"Andrew!" she called out. "Can you hear me? Help me! I'm down here in the tunnel and I can't get out!"

There was no reply.

She got carefully up off the ground. She was not badly hurt. No broken bones. She raised one hand and could feel the cold roof of a tunnel above her head. So she had found the tunnel. What now? She would just have to wait until Andrew got help. He would know what had happened. Or would he? How much had he seen? Had he seen her slip into the old tunnel which they had been looking for? The tunnel from the tower to Cliff House? Or had he thought she had fallen off the cliff into the sea?

Of course he had seen what had happened! He would get help and they would soon move the big rock that was blocking the hole in the tunnel roof. They would soon get her out into the sunshine again.

Until then, she would explore the tunnel. She could see nothing, but she could use her hands to feel the way.

Slowly she felt her way along one side of the tunnel until she came to a wall across the end. The wall which Reuben had built, of course. Then she moved across to the other side and began to go back the way she had come. Halfway down the tunnel she suddenly felt something under her foot. It was not a stone. She bent down and reached out for it. It was a round stick. Perhaps she could use it for something. Perhaps she could move the big rock with it. She took hold of the end of the stick with her other hand – and dropped it with a scream of horror.

It was not a stick. It was a bone! A human leg-bone!

*

Two policemen were carefully moving the rocks and stones to one side when Mr Martinez and Johnny Weddell ran up to help them.

"Be careful," said one of them. "We don't want another accident! The Heavy Rescue people are on their way. They'll be here soon."

"Are you sure she didn't fall down the cliff?" asked Mr Martinez.

"Not much rock has actually slipped down the cliff face," said Johnny, throwing a heavy stone to one side. "This is where the old tower stood. We think most of the rock has fallen into the cellar where the tunnel was."

They worked as quickly as they dared and as carefully as they could for ten minutes. Then at last they came to the large rock which had fallen over the hole in the roof of the tunnel. Very carefully they tried to lift it, but it was too heavy. They could see that the rock was lying on the top of

the cellar wall of the old tower. As one of the policemen moved his feet, several more small stones fell into the tunnel, and a small hole appeared.

"Jenny!" shouted one of the policemen to the policewoman. "Bring a torch from the car and send those people away! Keep the road clear for the Heavy Rescue truck. Where the hell is it, anyway?"

The policewoman brought the torch and they shone it down into the blackness. It was the tunnel all right. They could see the floor and walls.

"Hello!" shouted the policeman with the torch. "Is there anyone down there?"

"Yes!" cried a small voice, and a few seconds later the torch was shining down on a very dirty face with very frightened eyes. "I'm OK now, but get me out of here quickly, please. I'm not alone."

"Not alone?"

"No. I think I've found Jonathan Martinez – or at least his bones. But there's no sign of the treasure."

"Treasure? What treasure?"

"The treasure my grandfather was looking for. The big black box full of Spanish gold."

Chapter 9 Answers to every question

"It was horrible, Andrew!" said Liz the following day, when she and her grandfather were sitting beside Andrew's bed in Truro General Hospital. "There I was in the dark with this 150-year-old skeleton!"

Andrew shivered, and smiled at her. "You were very brave!"

"I've told your mum and dad what's happened," said their grandad. "At first they wanted to come right down, but I told them that you were both OK, so they decided to wait until Saturday before coming. I hope they don't blame me for not looking after you properly. How's your head, Andrew?"

"It still hurts a little, but the doctor says it's nothing serious. A few stones were still falling when I ran up to see what had happened to Liz. One of them must have hit me on the head. Johnny Weddell found me. All I can remember is waking up in the ambulance! The doctor says I can go home tomorrow." He turned to his sister. "Did you really think that you would find a box full of gold in that tunnel, Liz?"

"No. But I had to be sure. I thought that I would find one of the Martinez twins down there. And I did. It was Jonathan, wasn't it, Grandad?"

"I expect so. I think you've already told us what must have happened, Liz. Before Aaron went off to Virginia in 1839, he came back to Portreath and tried to steal the gold. Perhaps he persuaded Jonathan to help him, but I don't think so. I think he killed Jonathan. The box was down in the cellar, of course, but he didn't find it. His father came down and discovered what had happened. He sent Aaron away to America and hid the gold beside his dead son. It was Jonathan's inheritance, after all. Aaron would have to look for it. Old Reuben even left a message on his grave to help Aaron find it."

It was now Liz's turn to shiver. "Horrible! Killing your own twin brother – for gold! How could anyone do that?"

"Your father was right, Liz," said her grandfather. "Gold drives men mad. They will do anything for it. I'm sure both of you must sometimes have thought that the idea of finding the family treasure was driving me mad," he said with a sad smile.

"Just a little mad, Grandad!" said Andrew, smiling back. "But what do you think happened to the gold? Did Aaron understand the message on the grave? Did he find the gold after his father's death? Did he take it back to the USA with him?"

"Not to the USA, Andrew. To the CSA."

"The CSA? What's that?"

"The Confederate States of America. Don't you remember? Aaron's farm was in Virginia. It was a tobacco plantation and he had many slaves to do the hard work on the farm. When Abraham Lincoln wanted to free the slaves, the southern states left the Union and there was civil war from 1861 to 1865. Aaron's father died in 1862. When Aaron came back to Portreath, he was a major in the Confederate Army. He was killed at the battle of Gettysburg the following year."

"How on earth did you find that out?" asked Liz in surprise.

"A kind young lady at the Public Records Office in Truro showed me how to use their computer. The information I had been trying to find for years was all there – on the Internet. I only had to type in 'American Civil War – Confederate Casualty Lists' and Aaron's name. I had the answer in a few seconds. 'Aaron Martinez, Major, 3rd Virginia Cavalry. Killed in Action, Gettysburg, July 2nd, 1863'."

Nobody spoke for a few moments. Then Andrew asked another question. "What gave you the idea that there was some connection between Aaron and the Civil War?"

"This," said Grandad, taking a small wooden box out of his briefcase. "I haven't shown it to Elizabeth yet." He turned to his granddaughter. "It was down in the tunnel, lying beside Jonathan's skeleton. Aaron must have put it there the night he came back. He exchanged it for the gold. He took the gold because his country needed it. He knew that it really belonged to Jonathan. He knew that everything would have belonged to the brother he had killed. That's why he was never seen again in Portreath. He gave up his inheritance without telling anyone and must have taken the next ship from Plymouth back to his new country. Would you like to open the box, Andrew?"

Andrew took the box and carefully opened it. There was no gold inside – just a bundle of old yellow papers. About thirty sheets. At the top of each sheet were the words: CONFEDERATE STATES OF AMERICA. LOAN, and underneath, in large letters, $1,000.

"What are they, Grandad?" asked Liz. "Are they banknotes or something?"

He smiled at her. "No. Not banknotes. They're loan certificates. Aaron must have exchanged all the money he had for them when the civil war started. The CSA needed money for their war against the USA. The only real money in those days was silver or gold coins. Aaron must have become a real Southern Gentleman in the twenty years he had lived in Virginia. Like most of the other rich farmers, he exchanged his gold for paper: loan certificates like these – a promise to repay the money if the CSA won the Civil War – which of course never happened. And when he heard that his father

LOAN

had died, he came back here for more gold, which he exchanged for these certificates."

"So these pieces of paper are not worth anything?" asked Liz.

"Don't look so sad, young lady! Each certificate is worth about £200 to a collector. I found that out on the Internet, too! The next thing I'm going to buy is a computer of my own!"

"But who do these certificates belong to?" asked Andrew.

"They belong," said Mr Martinez, looking at Liz with a smile, "to the finder!"

"But I didn't find them!" cried Liz.

"Yes, you did. And if you look inside the lid of the box, you'll find the words: 'For the heirs of Jonathan Martinez'. Jonathan is my name, too! It's a strange coincidence, isn't it? And nobody would have found the certificates if you hadn't found the tunnel. And I think you should have them. It's what you were looking for, isn't it? Buried treasure?"

"Not really," said Liz slowly. "I wasn't just looking for treasure. I was looking for the truth about what really happened." And she told her grandfather about her dream. And about going down into Johnny Weddell's cellar. And about the blocked-up doorway. "Johnny thought I was joking when I told him there was a ghost in his cellar, but I wasn't. I could feel it... and my dream... I had to find out the truth. Even if there was no big black wooden box filled with Spanish gold down there in the tunnel. Did I do right to want to find out the truth, Grandad?"

"Yes, Elizabeth," said the old man, putting his arm round his granddaughter's shoulders. "You did right."

Chapter 10 Spanish gold

Liz and Andrew enjoyed the last week of their holiday very much. Their grandfather took them to many interesting places, and the weather stayed fine. Mr Martinez seemed happier, too. He was no longer thinking about Spanish gold all the time. He no longer had that mad look in his eyes when they talked about it.

They contacted a collector in Plymouth, who paid them a good price for ten of the Confederate Loan Certificates. Liz had given Andrew and her grandfather five each and said she would keep the others to sell later – if she wanted to buy a car, or go to university, or something like that.

"You're lucky you didn't find any real gold," the collector told them.

"Why is that?" asked Mr Martinez.

"Well, if you had found a box of hidden treasure, it would have been a treasure trove. And a treasure trove belongs to the Crown. You get a reward for finding it, of course. But never the full value."

"So much for our Spanish gold!" said Mr Martinez with a smile.

They drove straight to a computer superstore and bought a computer with an Internet connection for Grandad.

Mr Martinez now had a new interest. His computer. He soon found out how to get onto the Internet and spent a lot of time in front of his computer for the next two days while Liz and Andrew enjoyed themselves down on the beach or up at the airfield with Johnny.

On the third day, Mr Martinez came running into the kitchen with a bundle of papers in his hand and a big smile on his face.

"I was right!" he cried. "Our family is related to the Martinez family of Portreath! It's all on the Internet! One of Reuben's younger daughters ran off with a man from Coventry. They had a child but never married, so their illegitimate son kept the name Martinez. Now I'm going to try and trace our family back to the Armada and Spain!"

Liz thought that she had never seen her grandfather so happy.

"What are you smiling about, young lady?" asked Andrew, trying to sound a bit like old Mr Martinez.

"Grandad doesn't know it," said Liz. "But I've got an even bigger surprise for him – for all of us!"

"What sort of surprise?" asked Andrew.

"I'm saving it for Saturday," was all that his sister would say.

*

On the Thursday, at a quiet little ceremony in St Mary's Church, Portreath, the bones of Jonathan Martinez were finally laid to rest beside those of his father Reuben.

"I wonder if Reuben ever knew the full meaning of the words on his own grave," said Mr Martinez.

"What do you mean, Grandad?" asked Liz.

" 'Only seek and you will find' was not just about the Spanish gold, Elizabeth. When Reuben discovered that Aaron had killed his brother – perhaps in a fight, perhaps even by accident – he knew that the only way to protect his other son was to hide Jonathan's body. He left it where he found it and blocked up both ends of the tunnel with the gold that really belonged to Jonathan inside. But he left Aaron a message on his grave: he told him to look for and find not only the gold but also his brother's bones. And it was you who found them, Liz, after all these years. You understood the message."

"Well," said Liz happily. "He was my great-great-great-great-great-great uncle, after all!"

*

"What an adventure!" said Mrs Martinez when she had heard all about what had happened. "I'll feel much better when you two are both safely back at school on Monday!"

"You've certainly made your grandfather happy," said their father. "I've never seen him so contented!"

"He's very busy with his new toy," said Andrew. "Grandad!" he called. "We're ready to leave now! Come into the kitchen and at least say goodbye to us!"

"Sorry," said old Mr Martinez. "I was just downloading something."

His son smiled. "Well, Dad, we're leaving now. Thank you for looking after the children. You must come and visit us in London in the summer. If you're not too busy with your new computer."

"Goodbye, Grandad," said Andrew.

"Just a minute!" said Liz. "I almost forgot. I've got a surprise for you all. Something I found down in the tunnel, when the daylight started coming in through the hole at the other end. They were lying on the ground. I went back and picked them up while I was waiting for the Heavy Rescue truck to arrive. I think I got them all..."

She put her hand in her jeans pocket and slowly laid five coins on the kitchen table.

Nobody spoke for a whole minute. The spring sun shone on the dull gold of five Spanish doubloons over four hundred years old.

They stared at the coins. They stared at Liz, wide-eyed and open-mouthed. Liz stared back, wondering what to say next.

"It's all that's left of the Spanish gold – the Martinez family treasure. There's only one coin for each of us, I'm afraid," she finally said. And when there was still no reaction from the others, she added, quietly: "Aaron must have dropped them. They must have fallen out of that big black wooden box."

Vocabulary

A

(to be) **afraid of sth.** Angst vor etwas haben
age Alter
airfield Flugplatz
alien ['eɪliən] andersartig; fremd
alive [ə'laɪv] lebendig; am Leben
ancestor ['ænsestə] Vorfahr/in
(to) **apologize** [ə'pɒlədʒaɪz] sich entschuldigen
Armada [ɑː'mɑːdə] *spanische Kriegsflotte, die England im Jahre 1588 angriff und in einem Sturm unterging*
astonished [ə'stɒnɪʃt] erstaunt
astonishment Erstaunen

B

bad luck Pech
battle Schlacht
beard [bɪəd] Bart
(to) **beg** betteln
(to) **belong** gehören
(to) **bend** (bent – bent) **down** sich bücken
blackness *hier:* Dunkelheit
(to) **blame sb.** jdm. die Schuld geben
(to) **blare** [bleə] plärren; heulen
(to) **block** blockieren
blocked-up blockiert
(to) **book** buchen
bored gelangweilt
at the **bottom** am Fuße; unten
brand Marke
briefcase Aktentasche
brown paper (braunes) Packpapier
(to) **build** (built – built) bauen
bullet Kugel
bundle ['bʌndl] Bündel
(to) **burn** (burnt – burnt) **down** abbrennen
(to) **bury** ['beri] begraben

C

Camborne ['kæmbɔːn] Kleinstadt in Cornwall
carriage ['kærɪdʒ] *hier:* Kutsche
case Etui; Schatulle
casualty ['kæʒuəlti] **list** Kriegsopferliste
cavalry ['kævlri] Reiterei; Kavallerie
cave Höhle
ceiling ['siːlɪŋ] Decke
cellar ['selə] Keller
ceremony ['serəməni] feierliche Handlung
certainly ['sɜːtnli] sicher; gewiss
certificate [sə'tɪfɪkət] Urkunde; Zertifikat
(to) **chase** jagen
cigarette [ˌsɪgə'ret] Zigarette
civil ['sɪvl] **war** Bürgerkrieg
(to) **claim** beanspruchen; in Empfang nehmen
clear klar; deutlich
(to) **climb** [klaɪm] klettern
clock Uhr

coach house Wagenremise
coin Münze
coincidence [kəʊ'ɪnsɪdəns] Zusammenfall
collector Sammler
Confederate States of America *die Südstaaten*
connection Verbindung
(to) **conquer** ['kɒŋkə] erobern
(to) **contact** ['kɒntækt] kontaktieren; in Verbindung treten
contented [kən'tentɪd] zufrieden
corridor ['kɒrɪdɔː] Gang
countryside Landschaft
crazy ['kreɪzi] verrückt
crop-spraying *das Getreide mit Unkrautvertilger besprühen*
the **Crown** der Staat (*verkörpert durch König oder Königin*)
cry Schrei; Ausruf
custom Sitte; Brauch

D

(to) **dare** wagen
daylight Tageslicht
(my) **dear** mein(e) Liebe(r)
disappointed [ˌdɪsə'pɔɪntɪd] enttäuscht
(to) **discover** entdecken
doorway Türöffnung
doubloon [dʌ'bluːn] (*spanische Goldmünze:*) Dublone
drawing Zeichnung; Plan
dreamer Träumer
(to) **drive** (drove – driven) **sb. mad** jdn. in den Wahnsinn treiben
dull [dʌl] matt, dumpf

E

Easter ['iːstə] Ostern
English Channel ['tʃænl] der Ärmelkanal
eldest älteste(r) (*bei Geschwistern*)
empty leer
(to) **enjoy oneself** Spaß haben
(to) **enter** betreten
equipment [ɪ'kwɪpmənt] Ausrüstung; Geräte
escudo *alte spanische Währungseinheit*
excited aufgeregt
except außer
(to) **exchange** [ɪks'tʃeɪndʒ] tauschen
(to) **explain** erklären
(to) **explore** erforschen

F

farmer Bauer; Landwirt
fascinated ['fæsɪneɪtɪd] fasziniert
feeling Gefühl
fence Zaun
fight [faɪt] Kampf; Schlägerei
finally zum Schluss
finder ['faɪndə] Finder
(to) **flash** blitzen
fleshless fleischlos
fog Nebel
(to make one's) **fortune** ['fɔːtʃuːn] sein Glück versuchen/machen
four-seater viersitzig
(to) **free** befreien
fresh frisch
fridge Kühlschrank

friendly freundlich
(to) **frighten** erschrecken

G

gate Tor
gentleman *hier etwa:* feiner Herr
generation [ˌdʒenəˈreɪʃn] Generation
glad froh
(to) **go mad** verrückt werden
(to be) **going on** sich abspielen
grandee [grænˈdiː] *spanischer oder portugiesischer Adliger*
grass [grɑːs] Gras
grave Grab
greenish grünlich

H

halfpenny [ˈheɪpni] halbes Pennystück (*vor Einführung der Dezimalwährung 1971*)
half-term Herbst- oder Pfingstferien (*mitten im Schultrimester*)
halfway auf halbem Wege
(to) **hang** (hanged – hanged) erhängen
hardly kaum
Hayle [heɪl] *Kleinstadt in Cornwall*
Heavy Rescue Team *etwa:* Technisches Hilfswerk (*als Rettungsdienst*)
heir [eə] Erbe/in
helpful hilfreich
(to) **hide** (hid – hidden) (sich) verstecken
(to) **hold** (held – held) **out** *hier:* ausstrecken
horror [ˈhɒrə] Entsetzen
Hugh [hjuː] **Town** *Hauptort der Scilly-Inseln*
(to) **hunt** jagen
hunting gun Jagdgewehr
in a **hurry** [ˈhʌri] in Eile

I

ideal [aɪˈdiːəl] ideal
illegitimate [ˌɪləˈdʒɪtəmət] außer-/unehelich
(to) **imagine** sich vorstellen
inheritance [ɪnˈherɪtəns] Erbe
inside (nach) innen
interest [ˈɪntrəst] Interesse
interested [ˈɪntrəstɪd] interessiert
interesting [ˈɪntrəstɪŋ] interessant

J

(to) **joke** spaßen

K

Keep off! Betreten verboten!
kind nett; freundlich

L

Lands End *äußerste Südwestspitze der englischen Küste*
lawyer [ˈlɔːjə] Rechtsanwalt
(to) **lay sb. to rest** jdn. beisetzen
(to) **lead** [liːd] (led – led) leiten; führen
(to) **let** (let – let) **go of** loslassen
lid Deckel
(to) **lie** (lay – lain) liegen
(to) **lift** heben

lighthouse Leuchtturm
lip Lippe
loan [ləʊn] Darlehen
(to) **look after sb.** auf jdn. aufpassen
loose [lu:s] lose
low niedrig

M

mad verrückt; wahnsinnig
major ['meɪdʒə] Major
(to) **march** marschieren
in **memory** of zum Andenken an
metal detector Metallsuchgerät
(to be) **missing** fehlen; vermisst sein
mist leichter Nebel
moonlight Mondlicht
musket ['mʌskɪt] Flinte; Muskete
mystery ['mɪstri] Geheimnis

N

navy ['neɪvi] Kriegsflotte
nobleman Adliger
normal ['nɔ:ml] normal
notebook Notizbuch
(to) **notice** bemerken

O

office Büro
once [wʌns] einmal
on one's own allein
opening Öffnung
open-mouthed mit offenem Mund
ourselves uns (selbst)
outside draußen; nach außen

P

parcel ['pɑ:sl] Paket
path [pɑ:θ] Pfad
Penzance [pen'zæns] *südwestlichste Stadt Cornwalls*
permission [pə'mɪʃn] Erlaubnis
(to) **persuade** [pə'sweɪd] überreden; überzeugen
pier [pɪə] Seesteg; Landungssteg
pile Haufen; Stapel
pilot ['paɪlət] Pilot
plantation [plɑ:n'teɪʃn] Plantage
pleasure ['pleʒə] Freude; Vergnügen
My **pleasure!** Gern geschehen! Ganz meinerseits!
plenty of jede Menge
Plymouth ['plɪməθ] Hafenstadt in Devon an der Südküste Englands
pocket Tasche (*in einem Kleidungsstück*)
Portreath [pɔ:'tri:θ] kleine Stadt an der Westküste Cornwalls
postmaster Postmeister
prisoner of war Kriegsgefangener
probably wahrscheinlich
promise Versprechen
(to) **promise** versprechen
properly richtig
(to) **protect** schützen
Public Records Office Stadt-/Staatsarchiv

R

RAF [ˌɑ:r eɪ 'ef] (= Royal Air Force) königliche Luftwaffe
reaction [ri'ækʃn] Reaktion

(to) **realize** ['rɪəlaɪz] sich einer Sache bewusst werden
Redruth [ˌred'ru:θ] Stadt an der Westküste Cornwalls
(to) **repay** zurückzahlen
(to) **reply** antworten
reward Belohnung
rich reich
(to) **ring** (rang – rung) klingeln
rocky felsig
roof Dach
ruin ['ru:ɪn] Ruine

S

Scilly ['sɪli] **Islands** *Inselgruppe südwestlich von Lands End*
scream Schrei
secret Geheimnis; Geheim-
section ['sekʃn] Abschnitt
(to) **seek** (sought [sɔ:t]– sought) *altmodisch:* suchen
sense Sinn
serious ['sɪəriəs] ernst
shadow Schatten
sharp scharf
sheet *hier:* Blatt
(to) **shine** (shone – shone) scheinen
(to) **shiver** zittern
shocked schockiert
shoulder ['ʃəʊldə] Schulter
silence ['saɪləns] Stille; Schweigen
silver Silber
(to) **sink** (sank – sunk) sinken
siren ['saɪrən] Sirene
skeleton ['skelɪtn] Skelett
slave Sklave/in
(to) **slide** (slid – slid) gleiten; rutschen
(to) **slip** (aus)rutschen
(to) **smoke** rauchen
smuggler ['smʌglə] Schmuggler
smuggling ['smʌglɪŋ] Schmuggeln
soldier ['səʊldʒə] Soldat
(to) **solve** lösen
somehow irgendwie
somewhere irgendwo
southern ['sʌðən] südlich
Spaniard ['spænjəd] Spanier
(to) **spend** (spent – spent) ausgeben (Geld); verbringen (Zeit)
(to) **spoil** verderben
spring Frühling
square quadratisch
stairs [steəz] Treppe
(to) **stare** anstarren
(to) **steal** (stole – stolen) stehlen
stick Stock
St Mary's *Hauptinsel der Scilly Islands*
St Michael's Mount *Insel vor der südlichen Küste von Cornwall*
stormy stürmisch
strange seltsam
stranger Fremde(r)
summerhouse Sommerhaus
sunshine Sonnenschein
superstore großes Kaufhaus oder Supermarkt
surely sicher; gewiss
surprise Überraschung
surprised überrascht
sweet süß
(to) **switch on** an-/einschalten

T

(to) **tear** [teə] (tore – torn) auf-/zerreißen
tip Spitze
tired ['taɪəd] müde
tobacco [tə'bækəʊ] Tabak
torch Taschenlampe
tourism ['tʊərɪzəm] Tourismus
(to) **trace** zurückverfolgen
tradition [trə'dɪʃn] Tradition
treasure ['treʒə] Schatz
treasure trove [trəʊv] (herrenloser) Schatzfund
truck Lastwagen
Truro ['trʊərəʊ] *Hauptstadt der Grafschaft Cornwall*
(to) **trust** vertrauen
truth [tru:θ] Wahrheit
tunnel ['tʌnl] Tunnel
twice [twaɪs] zweimal

U

unconscious [ʌn'kɒnʃəs] bewusstlos
underground unterirdisch
underneath unterhalb von
university [ˌju:nɪ'vɜ:səti] Universität
(to) **upset** [ʌp'set] (upset – upset) beunruhigen; aus der Fassung bringen

V

valuable ['væljuəbl] wertvoll
value ['vælju:] Wert
visitor Besucher

W

(to) **wander** ['wɒndə] wandern; umherirren
at **war** im Kriegszustand
warning Warnung
(to) **waste** verschwenden
(to) **wave** winken
What on earth ...! Was in aller Welt ...!
Where the hell ...! Wo um Himmels Willen ...!
wide weit
wide-eyed mit weit geöffneten Augen
(to) **wonder** ['wʌndə] sich fragen
wonderful wunderbar
wooden ['wʊdn] aus Holz gemacht; hölzern
worn abgenutzt

Y

yourself dich/euch/sich selbst

Questions and Activities

Before you start

Use the Internet or other sources to find out something about:

1 Cornwall
2 Spanish gold doubloons
3 The Spanish Armada of 1588
4 Sir Francis Drake

Then write a few sentences about each topic.

Chapter 1: Grandad's story

1 Did you find anything out about Cornish history in this story which you didn't already know? Write three short sentences beginning with: I didn't know…, It was new to me that…, I was unaware that…
2 Do you think the old Castilian tradition of leaving the farm to the eldest son was fair? Give your reasons.
3 In these days of emancipation, there are still some examples of unfair treatment of women. Write down as many as you can think of.
4 What started the trouble between Reuben Martinez's sons?
5 What do you think happened to Jonathan and Aaron Martinez? Any ideas yet?

Chapter 2: Dad's story

1. It was only in 1971 that Britain introduced decimal currency (£1 – 100p) for the first time. What were the units of currency before 1971? Look up shilling on the Internet and look at the article in Wikipedia, the free encyclopedia. You will find the answer there.
2. Which of the two stories in Chapter 1 (Grandfather's story) and Chapter 2 (Dad's story) did you enjoy better? Give one or two reasons for your choice.
3. Why do you think Dad didn't tell Liz and Andrew the stories about the Spanish gold and the Martinez family?
4. What big difference do you discover between old Mr Martinez and the father of Liz and Andrew?
5. What warning does Dad give to his children? Do you think he is right?

Chapter 3: Easter at Portreath

1. Portreath is the name of a real place in Cornwall. You will find photos of it on the Internet. Would you like to spend a holiday there? Have a good look at the photos of Portreath and give three good reasons why or why not.
2. Can you find any hints in this chapter that anything strange might happen to Liz or Andrew?
3. What have you discovered in the first three chapters about Cornish people and superstition (Aberglaube)?
4. Do you believe in ghosts? Give two reasons why or why not!

5 "Jon Martinez is just a dreamer!" says the postmaster. What do you think old Mr Martinez is 'dreaming' about?

6 What has he done in his life so far to realize his dreams? Name at least two things which he has done.

Chapter 4: Seek and you shall find

bis Mi

1 Have you ever flown in a small aircraft like Liz and Andrew? If you have, write a few sentences about it. If you haven't, write a few sentences about your last flight in a big aircraft!

2 Later that day, Liz wrote a letter home to her parents and told them about Grandad's surprise. Write her letter for her! Say where they went and what they saw.

3 Do you think Liz and Andrew are interested in the 'family graves'? Give two or three reasons why or why not.

4 A little grammar practice: look at the words on Reuben Martinez's gravestone. In old-fashioned English and in poetry, the grammar is a bit different from modern English. Some things are missing, aren't they? Re-write the inscription on the gravestone using the same words but modern English grammar.

5 Liz suddenly seems to know a lot about the Martinez family history. Where do you think she gets her information from?

6 What do you think is the significance of Reuben's grave at the end of this chapter?

7 Why is Liz so upset?

Chapter 5: The missing tower

1 Why does Grandad tell Andrew not to tell his parents about what happened to Liz that afternoon?
2 Where do you think Mr Martinez's thoughts are leading him?
3 Would you tell your parents what had happened that day if you were Andrew? Give your reasons.
4 Do you like museums? Write a few sentences about your last museum visit.
5 England was last conquered by the Normans in 1066. In what way could this explain Andrew's feelings about the 'alien culture' of Spain?
6 Do you have the same feelings about your own country?
7 What strange thing happens to Liz in the museum?
8 Why is Andrew so astonished when he watches Liz looking at the old photo in the museum?
9 Why do you think old Mr Martinez is so quiet on the way back from Truro?
10 Why doesn't Liz want to tell her grandfather about her dream?

Chapter 6: Two strange dreams

1 Do you sometimes have strange dreams? Would you like to write one of them down?
2 Explain what is happening in Liz's dream in your own words.
3 Are there any connections between the two dreams? Find as many as you can and write them down.

Chapter 7: Ghost hunt

1 What do you think was in the plane which Andrew heard in the night?
2 Why does Andrew wish he had not seen what had happened to one of the brown-paper parcels?
3 Do you think Liz really needs to go to the toilet? What do you think she is doing during those ten minutes?
4 What do you think Johnny Weddell is worrying about while Liz is out of the office?
5 Why does Liz say she wants to see the old cellars? Is this her real reason?

Chapter 8: On the cliffs

1 Why is Andrew angry with Liz at first?
2 Liz thinks the secret of the Martinez family is in the old tunnel. What do you think is in the tunnel?
3 This long chapter is divided into sections. The order of what happens in the story seems to be mixed up: the story is not told 'in a straight line'. Why do you think that the author does this?
4 In many stories, the reader knows more about what is happening than the people in the story. Is this true in this chapter? What effect does this way of telling the story have on the reader?
5 Liz thinks that Andrew will fetch help. From the reader's point of view, would you say that Liz's thoughts are:
* optimistic?
* silly?
* ironic?
* pessimistic?

Explain your opinion in a sentence or two. Now do the same from Liz's point of view.

Chapter 9: Answers to every question

1 Make a list of the questions which are answered in this chapter and give the answers.
2 Do you yourself have any questions which are not answered at the end of the story? If you are working in a group, ask the others your questions and talk about the answers.
3 Find out more about the American Civil War, its causes and its results. The Internet will help you here.
4 What changes do you notice in old Mr Martinez towards the end of this chapter?

Chapter 10: Spanish gold

1 Why were they lucky not to find a box full of gold?
2 Why is Grandad so busy during the last week of the holiday?
3 How much do you know about your own family history? Write down the most important facts in a few sentences.
4 Had you guessed Liz's surprise before you reached the end of the story? Be honest! What did you think it was?

After reading the story

1 Did you enjoy the story? Talk about it with the others if you are working in a group. What did you enjoy most – or least?

2 Various people are looking for different things in this story. Who is looking for what?
3 Would you call 'Spanish Gold' a ghost story? How would you describe it?
4 Talk to the others in your group about the type of stories you enjoy reading or about the types of TV programmes or films you like watching. If you are not working in a group, write down a few sentences about your favourites.